This book belongs to

_____

Thank You for Your Purchase!

We are delighted that you have chosen our coloring book to enrich your daily life. By choosing to engage with our art, you are stepping into a world of relaxation, creativity, and mindfulness.

We hope this coloring book brings you joy and tranquility as you explore the intricate designs and vibrant possibilities within its pages.

Share your designs with your loved ones or think of it as a present that offers mindfulness and a touch of personal creativity, perfect for anyone in your life who appreciates a peaceful escape.

Happy coloring!

We'd Love to Hear from You!

Your feedback is incredibly important to us and helps us continue to improve and provide the best possible products to our customers. If you have a moment, please leave a review on Amazon. Sharing your experience not only supports us, but it also helps fellow coloring enthusiasts make informed decisions.

How to Leave a Review:

1. Go to the product page on Amazon.
2. Click on 'Customer Reviews' next to the star rating.
3. Click 'Write a customer review' and share your thoughts!

It doesn't take long, and every review truly makes a difference. Plus, we love hearing about the beautiful artwork you create!

Garden flowers

Tulips

Peonies

Hortensias

Orchid

Irises

Calla Lilies

Phlox

Geranium

Gladiolus

Petunias

Zinnias

Delphinium

Gerbera Daisies

Cornflowers

Alstroemerias

Agapanthus

Freesias

Liatrus

Gypsophila

Eryngium

Campanula

Celosia

Dianthus

Astilbe

Gardenia

Marigold

Dahlias

Lavender

Sunflowers

Roses

Lotuses

Frangipani

Fuchsia

Saffron Crocus

Lilac

Cherry Blossom

Hyacinth

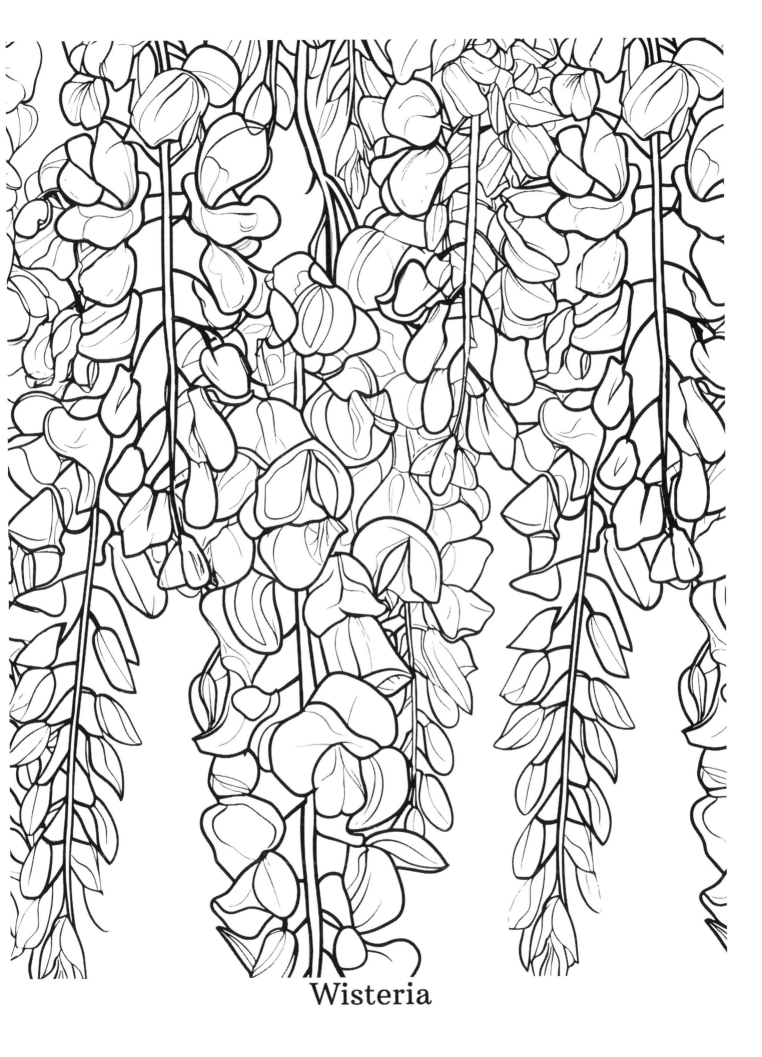

Wisteria

Magnolia

Hibiscus

Daffodil

Calendula

Poppy Flower

Borage

Lily of the Valley

Cyanus

Aster Flower

Harebell Flower

Made in the USA
Columbia, SC
05 September 2024

41790136R00057